I've Got a Tail!

FOR RICHARD —J.M.

FOR FREYA & ORTON —H.T.

Text copyright © 2020 Julie Murphy • Illustrations copyright © 2020 Hannah Tolson
Published in 2020 by Amicus Ink, an imprint of Amicus • P.O. Box 1329 • Mankato, MN 56002
www.amicuspublishing.us

Names: Murphy, Julie, 1965- author. | Tolson, Hannah, illustrator.
Title: I've got a tail! : terrific tails of the animal world / by Julie Murphy ; illustrated by Hannah Tolson.
Description: Mankato, MN : Amicus Ink, [2020] | Audience: Age 7. | Audience: K to Grade 3. |
Summary: "From dolphins with tails that spin to a viper whose tail looks like a spider, animals from around the world
describe how their tails help them survive. Covering adaptations to desert, ocean, forest, and arctic habitats, this narrative
nonfiction picture book highlights the diversity of the animal world"-- Provided by publisher. |
Identifiers: LCCN 2019016552 (print) | LCCN 2019020617 (ebook) | ISBN
9781681525044 (ebook) | ISBN 9781681525013 (hardcover)
Subjects: LCSH: Tail--Juvenile literature.
Classification: LCC QL950.6 (ebook) | LCC QL9506 .M87 2020 (print) | DDC 591.47--dc23
LC record available at https://lccn.loc.gov/2019016552

Editor: Rebecca Glaser
Designer: Veronica Scott

First edition 9 8 7 6 5 4 3 2 1 • Printed in China

I've Got a Tail!

TERRIFIC TAILS OF THE ANIMAL WORLD

BY JULIE MURPHY • ILLUSTRATED BY HANNAH TOLSON

amicus ink

Mankato, Minnesota

Tails can whip and drop, grip and prop.
Some tails swat, some tails sting,
some tails smell, and even . . . SING!

Animal tails do amazing things!

I've got a SHIMMERY tail!

My curly tail shines silver in the sunlight.

The male WILSON'S BIRD-OF-PARADISE
dances to show off his striking tail and
bright blue head. Will it be enough to
win a mate?

I've got a SPINNER tail!

My tail helps me spin like a ballerina as I leap high into the air.

A SPINNER DOLPHIN can twirl
up to seven times in one leap!

I've got a DROP tail!

My tail can fall off
if I'm attacked.

The DESERT NIGHT LIZARD leaves behind its wriggling tail to distract predators. This gives the lizard a chance to escape.

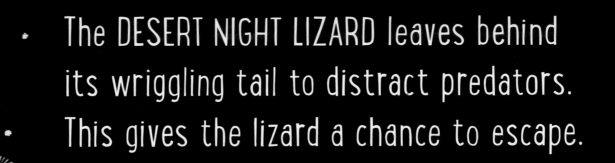

I've got a
PROP tail!

My tail has a spine that helps me
stand on the ocean floor.

The TRIPOD FISH stands as still as a statue on three spines. It waits for tiny, tasty creatures to pass underneath in the current. Chowtime!

I've got a STINKY tail!

My tail is my smelly
weapon in stink fights.

Male RING-TAILED LEMURS hold their smelly tails high and wave them at each other. The male with the smelliest tail is the first to greet the females.

Beware, I've got a STINGING tail!

My tail has a pointy tip
that's packed with venom.

The SCORPION stings prey with its tail. Venom in the sting stops the prey from moving, so it's easier to eat.

I've got a SWATTING tail!

With a few quick flicks of my tail,
I send pesky insects packing.

A GIRAFFE uses its tail to help shoo away
disease-carrying insects before they
have a chance to bite.

I've got a SINGING tail!

My tail sings a love song
to help me find a mate.

Male ANNA'S HUMMINGBIRDS dive through the sky with their tails spread wide. Air passing over the tail feathers makes a special sound the females love.

I've got a COPYCAT tail!

The tip of my tail looks
like a spider!

The SPIDER-TAILED HORNED VIPER hides in cracks, with its spiderlike tail poking out. The tail's tip wriggles. Hungry birds approach. But the birds don't eat—the snake does!

I've got a GRIPPING tail!

My tail curls around branches to keep me safe up high.

The COMMON RINGTAIL POSSUM holds on tight with its tail and back feet, while its front paws pick leaves, fruit, and flowers to eat.

I've got a KNOCKOUT tail!

My super-long tail works like a
whip to make catching food a *snap*.

The THRESHER SHARK hunts inside a ball of sardines. One swipe of its tail can knock out up to seven fish. Now that's fast food!

I've got a SNUGGLY tail!

In my home of snow and ice, my tail doubles as a soft, warm blanket.

The ARCTIC FOX lives near the North Pole, where it gets colder than inside your freezer! But the fox sleeps wonderfully warm with its fluffy, wraparound tail.

Pets have tails too!
What can their tails do?

WHERE DO THESE ANIMALS LIVE?

Arctic fox

Anna's hummingbird

Scorpion

Spinner dolphin

Desert night lizard

Here are places where
you can find these animals. Some
can be found in other places too.
Do you know any other places
you could find them?

Spider-tailed horned viper

Thresher shark

Wilson's bird-of-paradise

Giraffe

Tripod fish

Common ringtail possum

Ring-tailed lemur

TRIPOD
FISH

DESERT NIGHT LIZARD

ARCTIC FOX

SCORPION

WILSON'S
BIRD-OF-PARADISE

SPINNER DOLPHIN